| PHOTO by

Acknowledgement

Page No. I Author/s I Title I Source I License

8 I Bram van de Sande I A beautiful autumn afternoon
https://www.flickr.com/photos/bramvdsande/24003454864/
Attribution-ShareAlike 2.0 Generic (CC BY-SA 2.0)

21 I Lenny K Photography I Swiss Landscape Remixed
https://www.flickr.com/photos/lennykphotography/24575918806
Attribution-ShareAlike 2.0 Generic (CC BY-SA 2.0)

23 I Pug Girl I Adelboden
https://www.flickr.com/photos/pug_girl/8628045491/
Attribution 2.0 Generic (CC BY 2.0)

33 I G.Lamar (gaylon-yancy.pixels.com)
Canadian Rockies (Alberta) I https://www.flickr.com/photos/geewhypics/50785422531/
Attribution 2.0 Generic (CC BY 2.0)

34 I G.Lamar (gaylon-yancy.pixels.com)
Farming I https://www.flickr.com/photos/geewhypics/49909418983/
Attribution 2.0 Generic (CC BY 2.0)

38 I paul bica
waipio valley I https://www.flickr.com/photos/dexxus/5499821986/
Attribution 2.0 Generic (CC BY 2.0)

39 I sagesolar
Churning the water, forceful and wild I https://www.flickr.com/photos/sagesolar/6807370614/
Attribution 2.0 Generic (CC BY 2.0)

40 i Adam
Solčava panoramic road - Klemenšek tourist farm I https://www.flickr.com/photos/aaddaamn/25314177117/
Attribution 2.0 Generic (CC BY 2.0)

www.ingramcontent.com/pod-product-compliance
Ingram Content Group UK Ltd.
Pitfield, Milton Keynes, MK11 3LW, UK
UKHW060112300726
14090UKWH00002B/143